Laughing Cat Publishing

www.laughingcatpublishing.com

The Shiny Bee

ISBN-13: 978-0-9995665-1-0

Text Copyright © 2018 Natalie Meraki

Illustration Copyright © 2018 Natalie Meraki

The Shiny Bee

Who Felt Out of Place

This book helps children (and adults) feel at home in their own skin. Everyone has felt like they don't belong. It is important to remember that not only everyone, but everything, is made of the same stuff. The shiny bee is family to the universe, and so are each of us.

TO THE WOMEN WHO HAVE LIFTED ME

HIGH ENOUGH TO SEE WITHIN.

Illustrated and written by

Natalie Meraki

This book belongs to:

_____

There once was a bee who
shined like the sun.

Some bees admired her, but some bees were
afraid of what they did not understand.
They wondered why she was different than them.

The shiny little bee felt out of place.

She didn't know how or why she shined—

she just shone.

One evening,
she sadly flew to the lake
and gazed at her reflection.

"What am I?"

the shiny bee wondered.

The lake reflected a clear night sky.

The bee looked up at the millions of shiny lights

just like her, but they were so far away.

Wait a second . . .

One seemed to be approaching.

Yes!

It was coming straight for her!

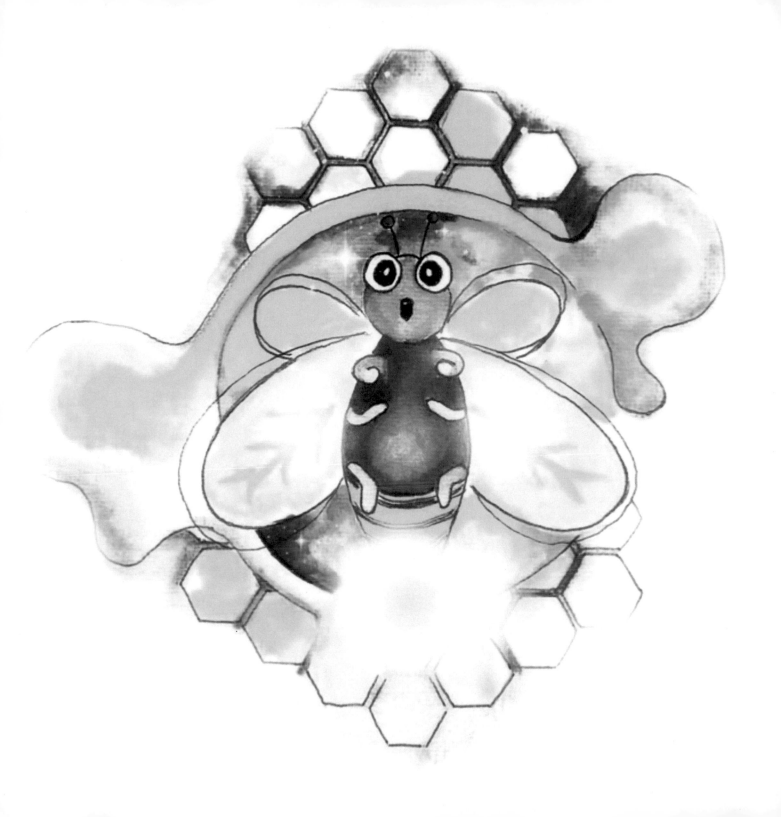

The shiny bee gulped several times . . .

and blinked her eyes a lot.

"Nice look on your face!

Now I know what it's like to be you."

"Come with me,
shiny bee!"

"I heard you wondering what you are.

You're a lot like me . . .

. . . I'M A SHINY STAR!"

"I'll take you through the
universe; it sings through
space and time."

"The universe is one big song; its message rings through humankind."

"Our galaxy is full of stars
and planets like that red one, Mars."

"Do you know

what it's all made of?

The same stuff as you.

The stuff we know and love."

"When a shiny star dies, it does not go away.

It's reborn into your eyes, in a nebula-like way."

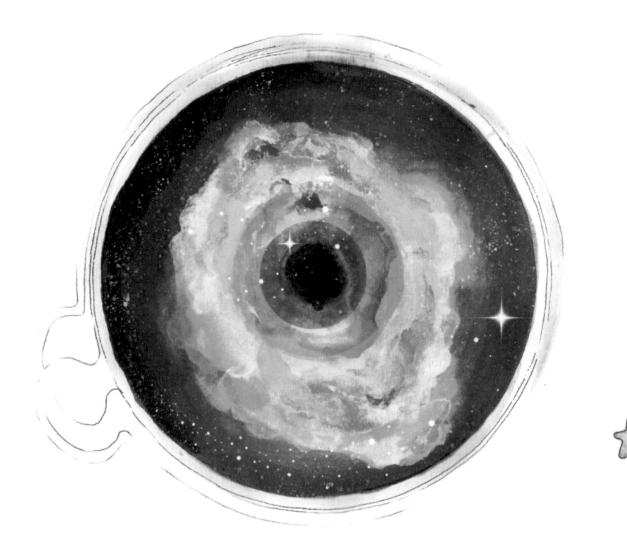

"Did you know that
all the elements in just one little hair
are in that asteroid way over there?"

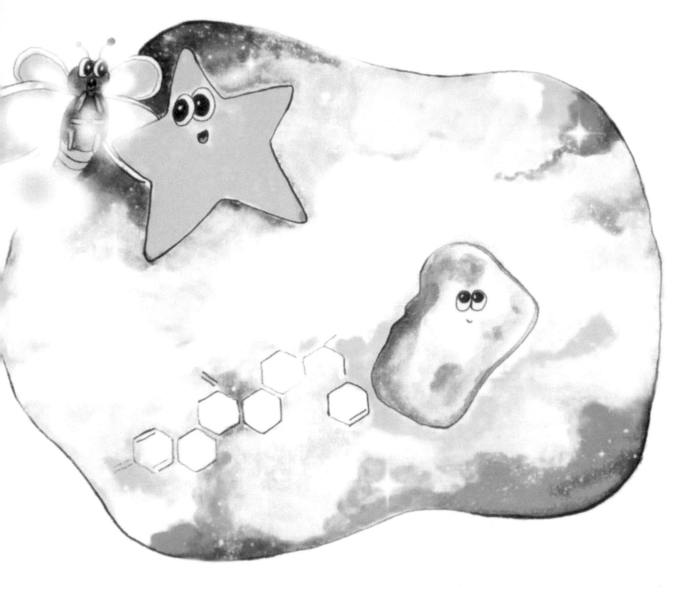

"Now here is a place that may

resonate with you.

That beauty is Earth,

and it's your home, too!"

"The ocean's like the universe;

it fills up empty space."

"You're a wave,

a part of it,

to always be embraced."

"You are in the universe.

It's also inside of you."

"The universe is in all things.

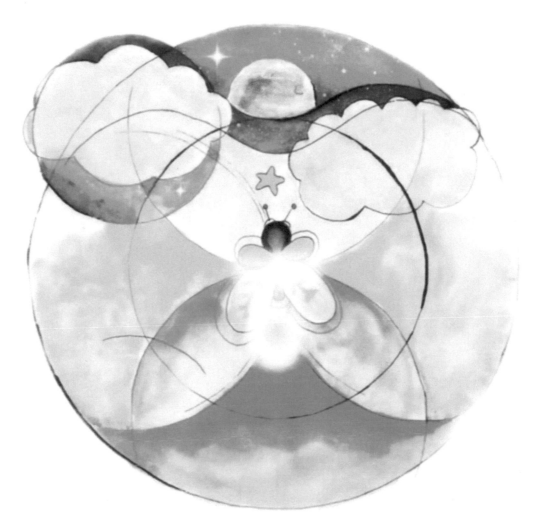

We're all connected, too!"

"So it really is alright if
you look or feel bizarre.
The truth is you belong
wherever, as whatever you are."

Made in the USA
San Bernardino, CA
15 September 2018